KU-506-931

BLACK BEAUTY

Anna Sewell

PICTURE CLASSICS

FROM HAPPY HOUSE BOOKS

 Published in the United States by Random House, Inc., New York, and simultaneously in Canada by Random House of Canada Limited, Toronto. Originally published by Pendulum Press, Inc., West Haven, Connecticut. Library of Congress Catalog Card Number: 80-53060 ISBN: 0-394-84716-4 Manufactured in the United States of America 1 2 3 4 5 6 7 8 9 0

BLACK BEAUTY

Picture Classics™ bring great works of literature vividly to life for today's generation of readers. The easy-to-digest, fun-to-read format puts new zest into masterpieces of adventure, mystery, science fiction, and other great stories.

about the author

Anna Sewell was born in Yarmouth, England, in 1820. As a result of a childhood fall, she was crippled for her short life.

During her early years, she spent many days taking her father to work. As she sat behind the horse she began to sympathize with it. The horse had no say in its plight. It was subjected to the fickle will of man. Miss Sewell wished that will to be a kindly one, and wrote *Black Beauty* to express her feelings.

The subtitle, *Autobiography of a Horse,* tells the reader that Beauty tells his own story. It is from his point of view that we see the pain of adjusting to a bit, of hauling a heavy load uphill, or of standing long hours in the cold.

One of Anna Sewell's biggest complaints concerned the restraining rein used by fashion-conscious horse owners. These reins were painful. Surprisingly, restraining reins were used on the horses in Anna's funeral procession. Her mother demanded that they be removed in a final tribute to the sympathetic voice of that unspeaking animal, the horse.

Anna Sewell

BLACK BEAUTY

Adapted by
NAUNERLE FARR

Illustrated by
RUDY NEBRES

a
VINCENT FAGO
production

Ginger
Squire Gordon
Black Beauty
Jerry
Mistress Gordon

"Men are strongest, and if they are cruel and have no feeling, there is nothing we can do, but just bear it." That is what my friend Ginger told me, but at first I was lucky.

In my time I have known many owners. . .thoughtless, cruel men and women, and kind and loving ones. I have pulled fine carriages, and poor wagons. I have even saved a life or two, as my own has been saved. And this is how it all began.

The first place I can remember well was a pleasant field with a pond and shady trees.

While I was young I drank my mother's milk, since I could not eat grass.

In the daytime I ran by her side, or played with the other colts. Sometimes we had rather rough play.

One day when there was a lot of kicking, my mother whinnied to me to come to her.

"Pay attention to what I am going to say to you. . .you have been well brought up."

"Your grandfather won the cup two years at the Newmarket races."

"Your grandmother had a very sweet temper, and you have never seen me kick or bite. I hope you will grow up gentle and good."

"Do your work with a good will, lift your feet up well when you trot, and never bite or kick."

Our master was a good, kind man. He gave us good food, a good home, and kind words.

Well, Dutchess, how is your little colt today?

One day he caught a boy throwing stones at the colts to make them run.

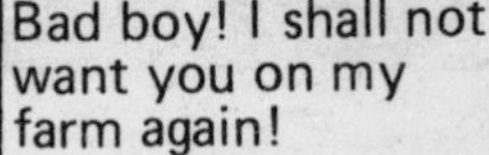
Bad boy! I shall not want you on my farm again!

One day when I was two years old, we heard a cry of hounds.

They have found a rabbit. If they come this way we'll see the hunt.
– Yo! Yo! Yo-o!

I watched in great surprise as the hunters appeared over the bank, jumped the stream, and came dashing across the field.

Near our end of the field, they jumped a high hedge.

One of the horses fell; he and his rider lay quite still on the ground.

*The young man was carried away and the veterinarian * was called to look at the horse.*

The veterinarian had said the horse had a broken leg. There was a big bang, and the horse lay still.

My mother seemed very upset. She said she never could see why men liked this sport, all for a rabbit they could get more easily some other way.

Not many days after, we saw a strange black coach pass by. It was carrying the young man to the cemetery to bury him.

* animal doctor

My master would not sell me until I was four years old. He said colts should not work like grown horses.

Yes, he will do very well.
I will break him in myself. I should not like him frightened or hurt.

The worst thing about the breaking-in was the bridle and bit. You can't think how unpleasant it feels, a great piece of steel pushed into your mouth.

But the master fed me oats and let me get used to it slowly.

Good boy! You must make the best of it.

Next came the saddle but that was not so bad. One morning my master got on my back and rode me around the field. I felt rather proud.

You go very well, Beauty!

The next difficult business was the horseshoes. The blacksmith took my feet one after the other.

Then I was taught to wear a harness, and I learned to pull a cart or carriage. My master often drove me in double harness with my mother.

In May a man came from Squire Gordon to take me.

Good-bye. . .be a good horse!

Next morning John Manly, the coachman, took me out to see me, and the Squire came to look at me, too.

Excellent. . .as fast as a deer, but well trained.

Next day the Squire took me out. When we returned I met my mistress.

Well, what shall we call him?

I think Black Beauty. . .for he is!

I had a fine box stall, the best in the stable. In the next stall stood a fat, gray pony.

How do you do?What is your name?
My name is Merry-legs. I carry the young ladies on my back.

Just then the head of a tall, good looking, brown mare looked over at me.

So it is you who has kicked me out of my box!
I have kicked no one out. The coachman put me here, and I wish to live in peace.

It was Merrylegs who told me that Ginger had been moved because of her bad temper. Then one day standing in the shade, Ginger spoke to me.

With your training I might have had a good temper. I never had anyone who was kind to me.

"My breaking-in was a bad time," Ginger said. "It was all done by force. Several men chased me into one corner of the field."

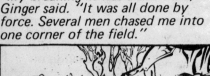

"One caught me by the hair on my forehead; another caught my nose; another twisted my mouth open."

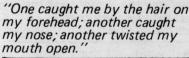

"There was a man called Samson who wanted to tire me out. He would make me run 'round in the field till he had worn me out."

"One day when I was already tired he climbed on me again, and put a new bit in my mouth. I stopped suddenly and he began to whip me."

"I began to kick and jump and we had a regular fight. He hit me with his whip but at last I threw him off backwards."

"I ran down the field and stood for a long time in the hot sun. Flies crawled all over my bleeding sides. At last Samson's father came."

"He was a fine old man with a kind voice. He led me back to the stable. Just at the door stood Samson, and I snapped at him."

You've done a bad day's work! A bad-tempered man will never make a good-tempered horse!

"I was sold to a London gentleman who knew nothing about horses and only wanted them to look fancy, so he drove with a tight bearing rein."

Tighter! I want her head held high!

"My neck ached, my windpipe hurt, I could hardly breathe. One day I began to jump and kick, and broke a lot of harness; so that was an end to that place."

"After another mean master, I was sent here. Of course it is different here, but who knows how long it will last?"

As the weeks went on, Ginger grew more gentle and cheerful.

I do believe this mare is getting fond of me.

Kindness is all she needs, poor thing.

One day in the late fall, I was harnessed into the small cart to take Squire Gordon on a business trip.

We went along merrily until we came to a gate and a low wooden bridge.

The river is rushing fast. I fear it will be a bad night.

When we started home in late afternoon, the wind had gotten very strong.
I wish we were out of these woods!

Suddenly with a crash a great oak tree fell across the road just before us!
That was a close call! Now what?

We must go around and use another road. It will be a good six miles to the bridge.
When we reached the bridge it was nearly dark.
There is water over the center of the bridge.
That happens sometimes during the floods.
The moment my feet touched the bridge, I knew something was wrong.
Come on, Beauty, what's wrong?
Go on, Beauty!
Hello there, hello, stop!

The bridge is broken in the middle! If you come on you'll be washed downstream!

John turned me gently to another road, and at last we came to the Hall again.

I've been so worried, my dear! Have you had an accident?

No, my dear. . .but if your Black Beauty had not been wiser than we, we should all have drowned at the wooden bridge.

After this, Ginger
and I drove my
owners to
visit some
friends who
lived far away.
The first night
we stopped at
a hotel.

Two stablemen came to take the horses. John stood by to see that we were properly rubbed down and cleaned.

A good-tempered animal.
He's been well trained.

After we had our corn, I went to sleep. But I awoke during the night uneasy. The air was thick and choking.

Someone shouted, "Fire!" A stableman rushed in and tried to lead out the horses but was so frightened himself, he fright-ened me more.

The horses won't come out.

Then I heard John's voice, quiet and cheery as always.

Come Beauty, we'll soon be out of this thick smoke.

Here, take this horse while I go back for the other.

John ran back into the stable. I set up a loud whinny as I saw him go.

There were smoke and flames, and something crashed. Then I saw John coming through the smoke leading Ginger.

My brave lad! Are you hurt?
N-no, sir. . . only filled with smoke!

The rest of the journey was easy, and in a few days we returned home. There, one night, I was awakened by the stable bell ringing loud.
John rushed in and almost before I could think he had the saddle on my back.
Wake up, Beauty. You must go fast now!
We found Squire standing at the Hall door.
Now, John, ride for your mistress's life. She needs the doctor right away.
I needed no whip or spur. I ran as fast as I could put my feet to the ground.

After an eight mile run, we drove up to the doctor's. John knocked like thunder at the door.

What is it?
Mrs. Gordon is very ill, sir. . .here is a note from Squire Gordon.

My horse has been out all day and is worn out. Can I take yours?
He ran all the way, sir, . . .but I am sure he will do his best.

When we reached the Hall, my master was at the door to meet us. He led the doctor inside, and Joe Green took me to the stable.

My legs shook under me, and I could only stand and pant. I had not a dry hair, and I was sweating all over.

Poor Beauty! You are so hot, I'll take care of you.

Joe was young and small, and knew very little, but I am sure he did the best he knew.

He gave me a pail of cold water, some hay and corn, and then went away.

Soon I began to shake, and turned very cold all over, especially my chest. I wished for John, but he had eight miles to walk, so I lay down and tried to sleep.

After a long while I heard John at the door. I gave a low cry. He was at my side in a moment.

Stupid boy! No blanket put on, and I bet he gave you cold water!

I was very ill for a long time. John took care of me night and day; my master, too, often came to see me.

My poor Beauty, my good horse, you saved your mistress's life!
I never saw a horse go so fast. He seemed to know what was the matter.

One night Joe Green's father was helping John to treat me.

I wish you'd say a kind word to Joe. The boy is heartbroken. He knows it was his fault, but it was only because he didn't know what to do.
He is not a bad boy. . .but that horse is my favorite. I will try to give Joe a good word tomorrow. . .if Beauty is better.

As for his not knowing what to do, he could have killed her, even though he didn't mean to.

But I got better and Joe Green went on very well; he learned quickly and was so careful that John began to trust him in many things. And after that, nothing made Joe as angry as to see a horse misused!

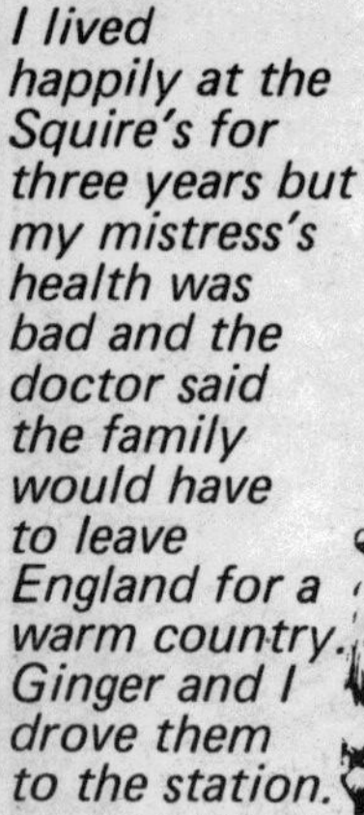
I lived happily at the Squire's for three years but my mistress's health was bad and the doctor said the family would have to leave England for a warm country. Ginger and I drove them to the station.

Good-bye, sir, and the best of luck to you both!
Good-bye, and thank you all!

Merrylegs went to the Blomefields with Joe Green to look after him.

Remember all I taught you.

Good luck, sir, and thanks.

Ginger and I were sold to the Squire's old friend, the Earl of W—. John took us to Earls Hall and handed us over to Mr. York, the Earl's coachman.

I don't believe there is a better pair of horses in the country. I am sad to part with them.

I should mention that we have never used the bearing rein with them.
If they come here they must wear it. His Lordship is reasonable but her Lady ship wants style!

A bearing rein is a short rein which keeps a horse's head up and its neck arched. When his Lordship came to look us over, York told him what John had said.

I think they will wear it if they're given a chance to get used to it. I'll talk to her Ladyship.

That afternoon we were harnessed to the carriage to take her Ladyship out. For the first time I wore a bearing rein. It was loose and not too bad.

Then we came to a high hill. I wanted to put my head forward and pull the carriage with strength from my whole body, but I had to pull with my head up, and the strain ended upon my legs and back.

Day by day our bearing reins were shortened. I began to be afraid of having my harness put on. Ginger, too, was restless.

Come now easy!

Then one day her Ladyship came down later than usual, and was angry.
Pull their heads high at once, York, and let us have no more of this nonsense!
The second York touched Ginger's rein to shorten it, she took her chance and kicked suddenly.
Quick! Watch it!
Ginger went on jumping, rearing, and kicking until at last she fell down.
Unbuckle the black horse! Unscrew the carriage pole! Cut the chain here!

Ginger was never put into the carriage again. One of the sons took her for a hunter. But I wore the short rein for four months, until Lord and Lady W— went up to London. Then I became the riding horse of one of the daughters, Lady Anne.

She was a fine horsewoman, riding sidesaddle as did all the ladies. We often went out with a gentleman called Blantyre, who rode a mare named Lizzie.
This Lizzie is a wonder. . .she's wonderful to ride and full of life.

One day Lady Anne ordered the sidesaddle to be put on Lizzie, and the other saddle on me.

What's going on?

I plan to try this Lizzie you praise so!

I intend to try Lizzie, so please help me to mount!
Please do not! She is too nervous for a lady!

In the village, Blantyre had a letter to deliver. He dismounted and hung my rein on the gate.

I will not be five minutes!
Don't hurry yourself. Lizzie and I shall not run away!

Just after he left, a boy came down the road with a group of colts, whipping them on. One of the colts came too close to Lizzie and frightened her.

Easy, my girl!

I tried to calm her.

But she began to run.

I gave a loud cry for help, and Blantyre came running.

He jumped into the saddle, and we chased after them.

The road ran straight for a mile and a half, then divided. . . .

Which way?
To the right! To the park!

This park was very uneven ground, a bad place for a running. We were catching up when they came to a stream.
Surely this will stop them!

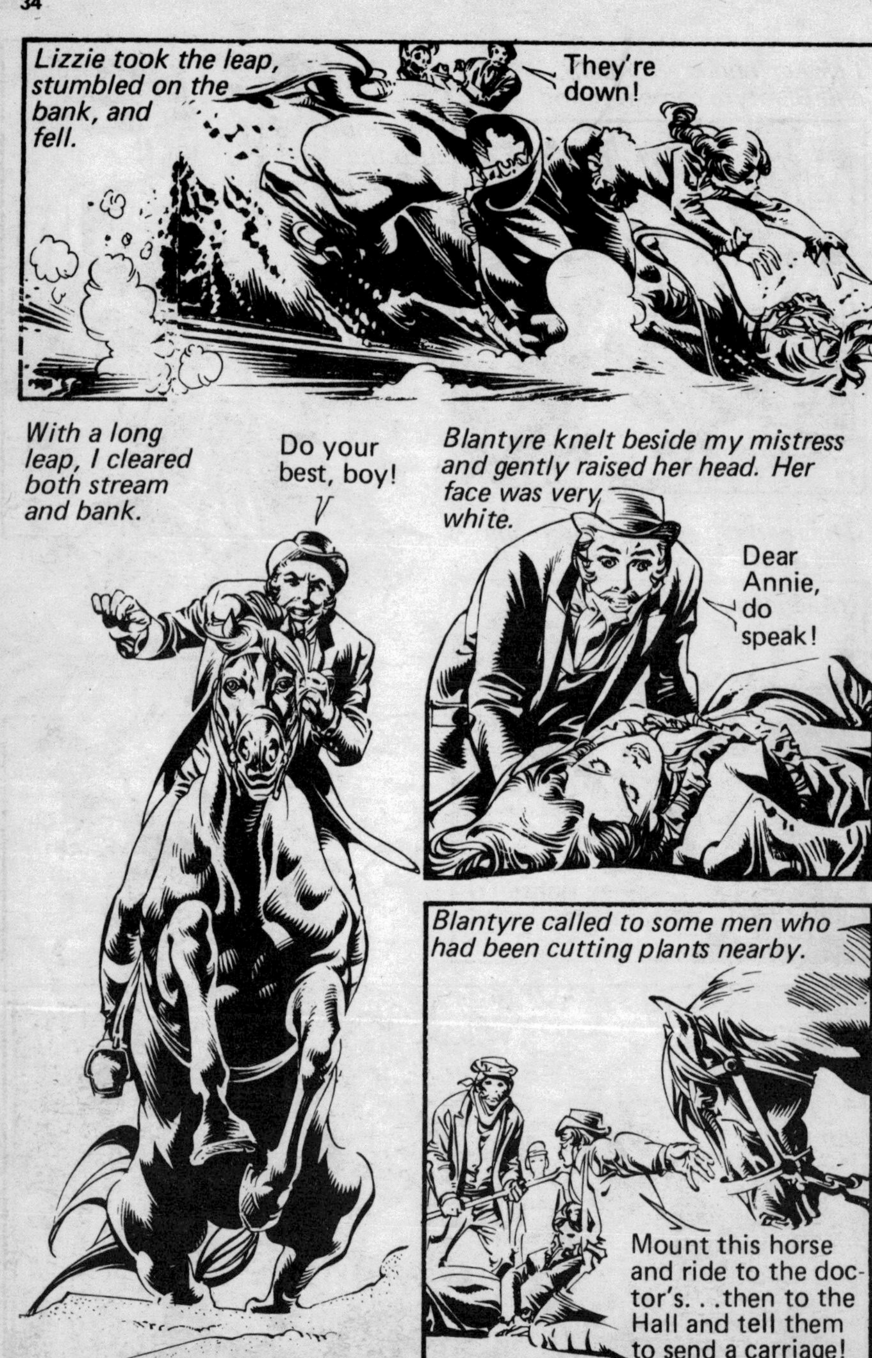
Lizzie took the leap, stumbled on the bank, and fell.
They're down!
With a long leap, I cleared both stream and bank.
Do your best, boy!
Blantyre knelt beside my mistress and gently raised her head. Her face was very white.
Dear Annie, do speak!
Blantyre called to some men who had been cutting plants nearby.
Mount this horse and ride to the doctor's. . .then to the Hall and tell them to send a carriage!

There was a great deal of rushing and excitement, during which I was taken back to my stable. Two days later Blantyre paid me a visit.

This horse knew of Annie's danger as well as I. I could not have stopped him.

Annie will soon be riding again, and she should never ride any horse but this one!

It was good news to learn that my mistress was recovering.

While York was in London with his Lordship, the stables were in charge of Reuben Smith. He was gentle and clever with horses, and everyone liked him. His one bad habit was he loved to drink; but he promised never again to touch a drop. One day he rode me to town and left me at the White Lion.

Feed him and have him ready for me at four o'clock.
Yes, Mr. Smith.

He did not call for me until nine o'clock and by then he was drunk!

There is a loose nail in one of your horse's shoes. Shall I take care of it?
Don't bother. I'll take care of it myself.

Where's my horse? Hurry up there and get him out!

Be careful Mr. Smith!
Mind your own business!

We were hardly out of town before he began to race, often giving me a cut with his whip.
Get on, you lazy animal!

The roads were stony. Going at this pace my shoe became looser, and soon came off. If he hadn't been drinking, Smith would have noticed something was wrong.
Over large, sharp stones, with one shoe gone, I was forced to run at my fastest speed. My foot hurt terribly, the hoof was split and the inside was badly cut.
Faster, you stumble-footed creature!
This could not go on; the pain was too great. I tripped, and fell hard on my knees. Smith was thrown off with great force.
I got up on my feet and limped to the side of the road. Smith groaned and then lay motionless.

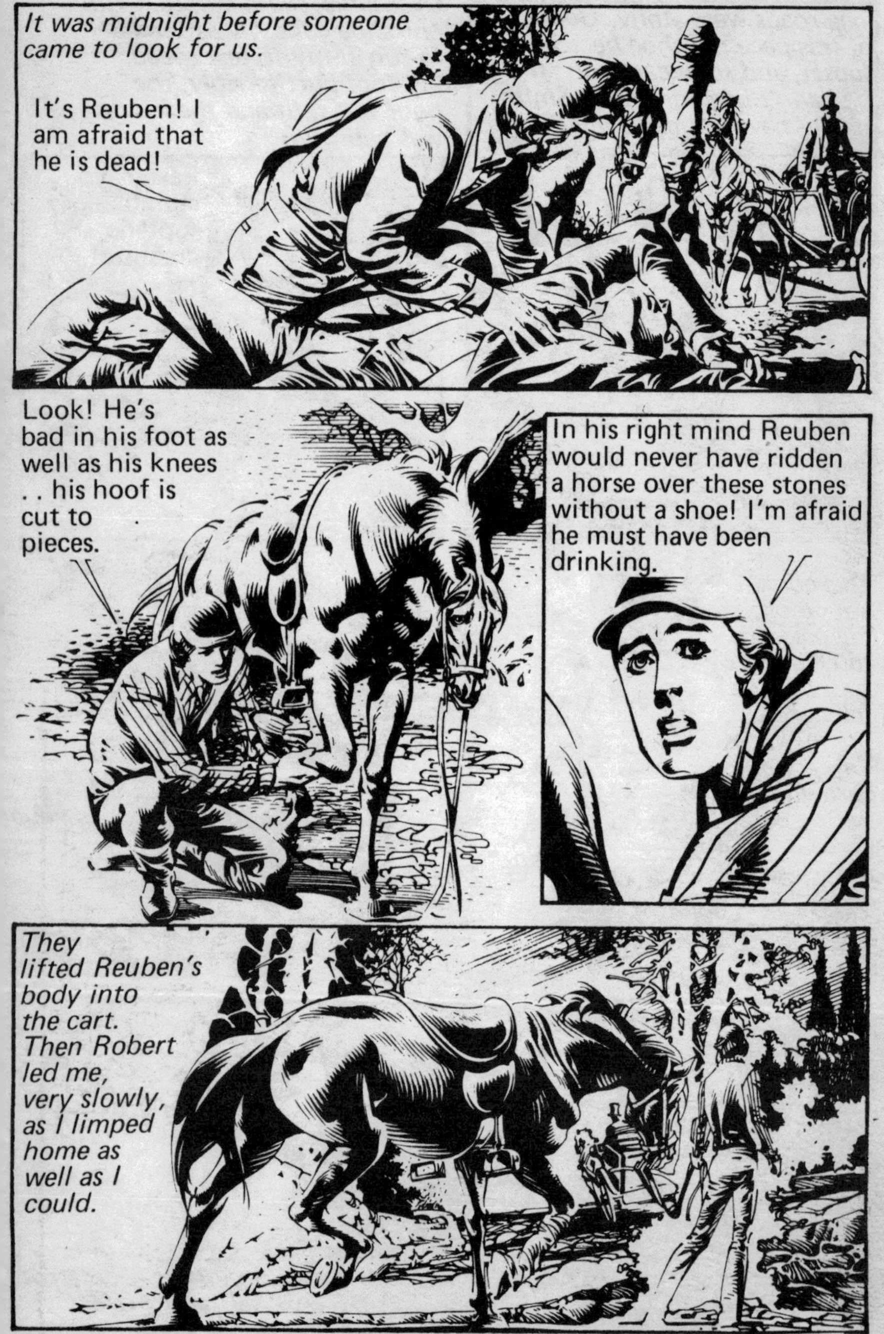
It was midnight before someone came to look for us.
It's Reuben! I am afraid that he is dead!
Look! He's bad in his foot as well as his knees . . his hoof is cut to pieces.
In his right mind Reuben would never have ridden a horse over these stones without a shoe! I'm afraid he must have been drinking.
They lifted Reuben's body into the cart. Then Robert led me, very slowly, as I limped home as well as I could.

At last I reached my stall. The veterinarian came, and started a long and painful treatment.

He should recover, but his knees will always have the scar.

Later, I was turned into a small meadow. One day, dear old Ginger was turned in to join me. At first I was happy to see her. . . .

. . . .but I was sad when I heard the reason. She had been ruined by young Lord George's hard and reckless riding.

Two fine horses, ruined in their prime. . .one by a drunkard and one by a fool!

I am sure Robert would not have spoken if anyone else had been there, but we heard him.

It is a pity but I could not have knees like these in my stables. He must be sold.

And so I was shipped to Bath and sold to the master of a renting stable there.

I was well fed and well cared for, but I was rented out to all kinds of people, and worked for all kinds of bad drivers.

The tight-rein drivers spoke of "Keeping the horse well in hand."

The loose-rein drivers paid no attention and let us stumble and go sidewise.

Then there was the steam-engine kind of driver, who wanted us to start off at full speed. . . .

Go along, you lazy beast!

. . . .and stop the same way.

Whoa, there, stop!

But there were good drivers, too. One of these, Mr. Barry, took a liking to me and got my master to sell me to him. He took me to a stable near his home.

I know little about horses but I want him well cared for. Plenty of oats, and beans, and bran. . . .

I thought I was lucky, but after a few days I didn't get as many oats.

In a few weeks I began to get weak. One day Mr. Barry rode me into the country to see a friend of his.

It seems to me your horse does not look as well as when you first had him.

He is not nearly as lively, but my groom tells me horses are always dull in autumn.

Autumn! Fiddlesticks! This horse is not being fed right! I think you should check into your stable. There are men bad enough to rob a horse of his food.

Could I have spoken, I could have told where my oats were going. Each morning the groom brought his small son in the oat bin.

Don't spill any. . . and take it straight home!

But my master checked, and a few mornings later, as the boy was leaving, two policemen walked in and took his arm.

We know your father keeps rabbits. Show us where he keeps the rabbit food.

He could not get away, and he led them to the bin.

There.
OATS

They found the groom in my stall.

Come along, it's all up!
I don't know what you want! I'm an honest man! The brat's lying!

They let the boy go, but they walked the groom away to the jail.

In a few days, my new groom came. He spent a great deal of time fixing his hair, whiskers, and necktie, before a little mirror in the harness room. It was always, "Yes, sir; yes, sir," to the master, and everyone thought Mr. Barry lucky to find him.

But he was a fake, the laziest groom I ever met. He didn't clean my feet, or check my shoes, or brush me well. He left my saddle damp, and my leather strap stiff.

One day Mr. Barry came in.

The stable smells rather bad. Should you not scrub that stall, and throw down plenty of water?

Well, sir, it is rather dangerous throwing down water in a horse's box. They are apt to catch a cold.

My feet became so sore from standing in my dirty stall, that I began to trip. Mr. Barry took me to the veterinarian.

This horse has the thrush, and badly. It comes from dirty stables where the straw is not properly cleaned.

With the right care I soon got better. But Mr. Barry was so mad at being twice fooled by his groom that he decided to give up keeping horses, and I was sent to a horse fair to be sold.

The gentlemen always turned away when they saw my knees.

I couldn't have such a blemished horse in my stables.

Some men examined me roughly as if I were a piece of wood.

I'll give you twenty-three pounds.

Not enough!

There was one soft spoken man I knew I should be happy with.

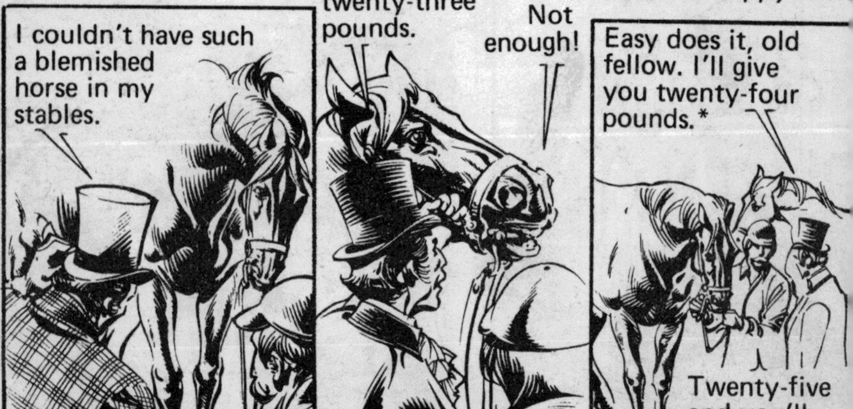

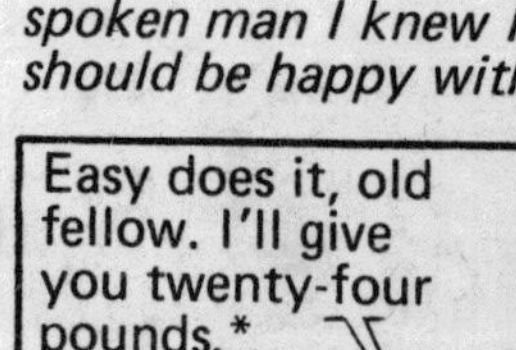
Easy does it, old fellow. I'll give you twenty-four pounds.*

Twenty-five and you'll have him!

* British money

Twenty-four ten and not another penny!
Done, and that's cheap for such a good horse.

The money was paid on the spot, and after feeding me well, my new master rode me away to London.

So, old chap, I think we'll suit each other very well!

After dark, we pulled up at a rather poor-looking house on a narrow street.

Oh, Jerry, you got one!
Open the gates, Harry, and bring a lantern.

Is he gentle, father?
Let me get him a bran mash while you rub him down.
As gentle as your own kitten Dolly. And a bran mash is just what he wants.

After a wonderful supper, I lay down in a warm, clean stall, feeling I was going to be happy.

My new master, Jerry Barker, was a cab driver who owned his own cab. I never knew a better man, nor a happier family than his.

He thought about his horse as much as he did for himself. One day two wild-looking young men came up to us.

Here, cabby! Go as fast as you can and get us to Victoria Station for the one o'clock train! A shilling extra.*

I will take you at the regular price, gentlemen. Shillings don't pay for rushing like that.

* British money

Take my cab, gentlemen!
Jerry won't go faster than
a slow, steady trot.

Whipping his tired horse, he set off as fast as he could.

No, old boy, a shilling would not pay for that sort of thing.

On Election Day there were terrible crowds and plenty of work. A poor young woman came along carrying a heavy child.

Please sir, can you tell me the way to St. Thomas's hospital?
Why, missis, you can't get there walking! It is three miles and that child is heavy!

You might be knocked down and the child run over. Get in the cab and I'll drive you there safe!

No, sir, thank you. I have only enough money to get back home.

Now get you into that cab, and I'll take you for nothing.

As Jerry went to open the door, two men ran up.

Here! Cab!
This cab is already reserved for that lady.
LONDON

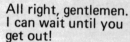

Lady? Oh, she can wait. Our business is very important.
Besides, we were in first.

All right, gentlemen. I can wait until you get out!

The men soon got out, calling Jerry all sorts of bad names, and we went on our way to the hospital.

Thank you a thousand times! I could not have gotten here alone.
You're welcome. I hope the dear child will soon be better.

Christmas is a merry time for some people, but for cabmen and their horses, it is no holiday. Often we have to wait for hours in the rain or frost.

Jerry's wife, Polly, worried about his health and always waited up for him.

I'll get something hot for both of you!

On New Year's Eve, we took two gentlemen to a house in the West End at nine o'clock.

Come for us at eleven. You may have to wait a few minutes, but don't be late.

As the clock struck eleven, we were at the door, but it did not open.

We'll have to wait, old chap!

It started to sleet and hail. It was very cold and there was no shelter. The clock struck twelve and then one.

The men came out at quarter past one, with never a word that they were sorry. My legs were frozen with cold and Jerry's cough was bad.

The same address where you picked us up, cabby.

When we got home, Jerry could hardly speak. Polly asked no questions, but opened the door for us.

I'll get Beauty something warm, and boil you some soup.

For several days it was the boy, Harry, who came to the stable. He took good care of me, but was worried and quiet.

How's your father, my boy?
Very bad. The doctor thinks it'll go one way or the other tonight.

But the next morning, the news was good.

Father is better. Mother thinks he will get over it!
Thank God for that! He's the best man I know.

Jerry got better, but the doctor said he must never go back to cab work again. One day while Harry brushed me, Dolly rushed into the stable.

Oh, Harry, the lady that mother used to work for writes that we're to go live near her in the country, and father will be her coachman!
It sounds great. . . except we'll have to sell Beauty!

Wanting me to have a good home, Jerry sold me to a corn dealer he knew. But the parting was a sad one for me.

Poor old Beauty. Dear old horse! I wish we could take you with us.

Unfortunately my new master had a worker who was always hurrying and rushing everyone.

Put on those extra bags, Jakes. No use going twice when once will do.
All right, but it's hard on the horse.

Jakes always had the bearing rein tight, which kept me from pulling easily.

One day I was loaded heavily and the road was a steep uphill. I used all my strength but I could not pull the load.

Get on, you lazy fellow, or I'll make you!

He was whipping me cruelly when a lady stepped up to him.

Please do not whip your horse anymore. The road is steep and I am sure he is doing his best.
If doing his best won't get this load up, he must do more than that, ma'am!

But is it not a very heavy load?

Yes, too heavy. But the boss put on the extra and I must do the best I can.

Let me take off this bearing-rein and he'll do a better job for you.
Well, ma'am, anything to please a lady!

The rein was taken off, and in a moment I put my head down to my knees. What a comfort!

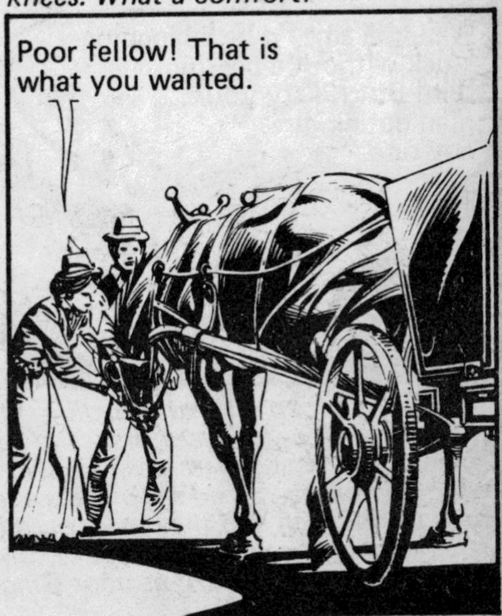
Poor fellow! That is what you wanted.

I put down my head and threw my weight against the collar, and pulled the load steadily up the hill. The lady walked along the footpath.

You see he was quite willing when you gave him the chance. You won't put that rein on again, will you?

Well, ma'am, I'd be a laughing-stock without a bearing rein! But I'll try your plan uphill, at any rate.
Thank you. I am sure you will find it better than the whip.

But no horse can take overloading. I became so weak that I was replaced with a younger horse and sold to a large cab owner, Nicholas Skinner. I had never known how terrible a cab horse's life was. Skinner had a bad set of cabs and a bad set of drivers. He was hard on the men and they were hard on the horses. And we worked seven days a week, in the heat of summer. But I still did my best and never held back; for as poor Ginger said, it was no use. Men are the strongest.

One day, when I had already done a good day's work, we picked up a family at the railway station.

Cab, here!
CABS

Papa, I am sure this poor horse can't take us and all our luggage. He is very weak and worn out.

Perhaps a second cab, sir, with so much luggage?—
Well, can your horse do it, or can't he?
He can do it all right, sir. Send up the luggage!

Papa, do take a second cab. I am sure it is very cruel.
Nonsense, Grace. Get in and don't make a fuss.

My gentle friend had to obey, and the luggage was loaded on top. The load was very heavy, and I had had a hard day.

I got along fairly well until we came to Ludgate Hill. I struggled to keep going.

Get up
with you!

Suddenly my feet slipped from under me and I fell to the ground heavily, knocking the breath from my body.

I could not move, I thought I was going to die. Someone untied my throat strap, and some drink was poured into my mouth. After a while, I found my life was coming back.

Finally I staggered to my feet and was led to a stable. A veterinarian looked me over.
This is a case of overwork.

If you could let him rest for six months, he would be able to work again.
I have no fields to nurse sick horses in. I work them as long as they'll go, and then sell them.

There is a horse sale coming up in ten days. If you rest him and feed him, you may get more than his skin is worth.

Ten days of perfect rest and good food did much for my health. Then I was taken to the sale, where I found myself in company with the old, broken-down horses.

There is a horse, Willie, that has known better days.

There's a deal of breeding about that horse.
Couldn't you buy him and make him young again, as you did with Ladybird?

My dear boy, I can't make all old horses young. Besides, Ladybird was not so very old.
Well, Grandpapa, I don't believe this one is old. Look in his mouth and you can tell.

The young gentleman's a knowing one sir. This horse is just overworked. It would be worth while to give five pounds for him and let him have a chance.
Very well. Take him to the inn.

And so I came to Thoroughgood's, to a better home than I ever expected to have again.

Give him hay and oats every night and morning, and the run of the field.
And you, Willie, must take care of him!

Willie came to see me every day, always with kind words and gentle petting. Sometimes his grandfather came, too.

He is growing young, Willie! By summer he will be as good as Ladybird!

the spring, Mr. Thoroughgood tried
e in the coach.

ow glad I am you
ought him, Grandpapa!
He has a beauti-
ful mouth, and
fine paces.

Now we must find him a
quiet home where he will
be taken care of. I think
the Blomefield's is the place.

ne day in
mmer
vas
rnessed
the
rriage
d driven
a pretty
ouse near
e village.

I feel sure he will be fine for
you ladies, Miss Blomefield
. . .but have him on trial
and see what your
coachman thinks.

the morning
young man
me for me.
hen he saw
y knees he
oked
isappointed.

I didn't think, sir, that
you would sell my
ladies a marked
horse like that.
You are only taking
him on trial. . .and I
am sure you will
like him!

I was led home and placed in a comfortable stable. The next day, while the groom was cleaning my face. . . .

This is just like the star that Black Beauty had. He is the same height, too. I wonder where Beauty is now.

A white star in the forehead, a white foot on the off side, and that little patch of white hair on her back! It must be Black Beauty!

Beauty, Beauty? Do you know me? Little Joe Green that almost killed you?

I put my nose to Joe to say we were friends. I never saw a man so pleased

Give you a fair chance. . .I should think so indeed! We'll have good times now!

ıat afternoon, Miss Ellen and Joe Green
ok me out in the carriage. I found she
ıs a good driver.

le seems
o be a
ine horse.
Indeed, ma'am. . .he is
Squire Gordon's old
Black Beauty!

I shall write to Mrs.
Gordon and tell her
that her favorite horse
has come to us! She
will be so pleased.

've now lived in this happy place
year. My ladies have prom-
sed I shall never be sold,
o I have nothing to fear. My
roubles are all over and
am at home.

THE END

fen, before I am quite awake, I dream I am still in Squire
ordon's orchard standing under the trees with my old friend.
only I could share my happiness with poor Ginger!